FRANCIS FRITH'S

A TASTE OF THE WEST MIDLANDS

THE FRANCIS FRITH COLLECTION

www.francisfrith.com

FRANCIS FRITH'S

A Taste of
THE WEST
MIDLANDS

Compiled by Julia Skinner

First published in the United Kingdom by
The Francis Frith Collection in 2012
Paperback Edition ISBN 978-1-84589-461-0

British Library Cataloguing in Publication Data

A Taste of The West Midlands
Julia Skinner

The Francis Frith Collection®
Oakley Business Park, Wylye Road,
Dinton, Wiltshire SP3 5EU
Tel: +44 (0) 1722 716 376
Email: info@francisfrith.co.uk
www.francisfrith.com

Printed and bound in England
Contains material sourced from responsibly managed forests

Front Cover: Market Drayton, Market Day 1911 63338t
The colour-tinting in this image is for illustrative purposes only, and is not intended
to be historically accurate.

CONTENTS

INTRODUCTION

—·—

Travel around the West Midland counties of England through the pages of this book and discover a selection of the delicious traditional food of the area, as well as some of the stories and fascinating facts behind the recipes. Your journey will be given added savour by the historical images taken by photographers from The Francis Frith Collection, showing the people and places of Herefordshire, Shropshire, Staffordshire, Warwickshire, West Midlands and Worcestershire in the past.

Regional traditional dishes were developed from the local produce that was available to thrifty housewives who had to feed large, hungry families on a limited budget. Many of the old recipes also reflect the limited cookery techniques that were available in the past, as well as the skills of the cooks who were able to provide cheap and tasty meals with only a fire, a skillet and a cauldron to cook with, often producing the historical version of 'boil in the bag' meals.

This book is not intended to provide a comprehensive collection of the local recipes of the region, and some recipes are modern interpretations using some of the fine local produce that this area is famous for, but we hope that the food described within these pages will provide you with a taste of the West Midland counties of England.

Coventry, Ford's Hospital
1892 30917

SOUPS AND SNACKS

—·—

RECIPE

—·—

Cream of Asparagus Soup

Worcestershire's Vale of Evesham is famous for its fruit and vegetables and especially for asparagus, which is in season from May to early July. Worcestershire asparagus has thin stems, unlike the fat green asparagus grown in East Anglia.

450g/1 lb asparagus spears
1 onion
25g/1oz butter
2 teaspoonfuls olive oil
150ml/ ¼ pint double cream
1 clove of garlic
A handful fresh green herbs such as chives or parsley, finely chopped
750ml/1¼ pints vegetable stock
Juice of half a lemon

Wash the asparagus spears thoroughly, to make sure any grit is removed from the flower head at the tip of each spear. Peel and roughly chop the onion, and peel and crush the garlic clove. Melt the butter in a large saucepan with the olive oil (this stops the butter burning). Add the onion and garlic and cook gently for 5 minutes. Chop the asparagus spears into chunks about 5cm (2 inches) long and add them to the pan. Continue to cook gently for a further 5 minutes. Add the stock to the pan, then cover the pan with its lid and simmer gently for 5-10 minutes, until the asparagus is soft. Remove the pan from the heat and allow to cool a little, then liquidize until it is smooth. If you like an even smoother texture the soup can be passed through a sieve. Add the lemon juice and the herbs to the soup and mix well. Season with salt and pepper to taste, then add the cream and reheat gently before serving – do not allow to boil.

—·—

RECITE

Bewdley Lentil Soup

450g/1 lb red lentils, washed and soaked for about 1 hour
1-2 large onions
2 tablespoonfuls of oil
3 crushed cloves of garlic
600ml/1 pint of chicken stock
1 teaspoonful of ground cumin
Half a teaspoonful of salt
Juice of 1 lemon
Fresh chives or parsley for garnish

Fry the onions in a large pan until they are soft and light brown. Stir in the crushed garlic. Add the lentils and the stock and bring to the boil, then reduce the heat, stir in the cumin and simmer for about 1½ hours, until the lentils have softened. Add a little more water during the cooking time if necessary. When the lentils are cooked, add salt to taste (salt should not be added earlier, as it will make the lentils tough). Just before serving, stir in the lemon juice. Serve piping hot in individual soup bowls, garnished with chopped chives or parsley.

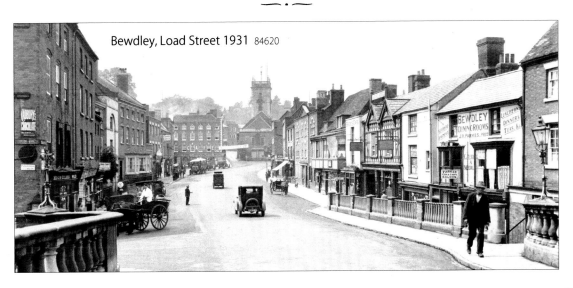

Bewdley, Load Street 1931 84620

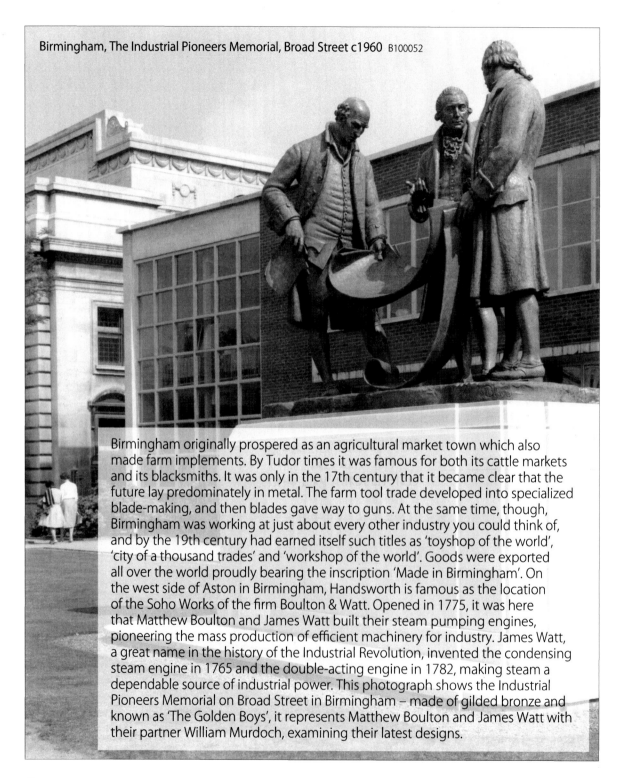

Birmingham, The Industrial Pioneers Memorial, Broad Street c1960 B100052

Birmingham originally prospered as an agricultural market town which also made farm implements. By Tudor times it was famous for both its cattle markets and its blacksmiths. It was only in the 17th century that it became clear that the future lay predominately in metal. The farm tool trade developed into specialized blade-making, and then blades gave way to guns. At the same time, though, Birmingham was working at just about every other industry you could think of, and by the 19th century had earned itself such titles as 'toyshop of the world', 'city of a thousand trades' and 'workshop of the world'. Goods were exported all over the world proudly bearing the inscription 'Made in Birmingham'. On the west side of Aston in Birmingham, Handsworth is famous as the location of the Soho Works of the firm Boulton & Watt. Opened in 1775, it was here that Matthew Boulton and James Watt built their steam pumping engines, pioneering the mass production of efficient machinery for industry. James Watt, a great name in the history of the Industrial Revolution, invented the condensing steam engine in 1765 and the double-acting engine in 1782, making steam a dependable source of industrial power. This photograph shows the Industrial Pioneers Memorial on Broad Street in Birmingham – made of gilded bronze and known as 'The Golden Boys', it represents Matthew Boulton and James Watt with their partner William Murdoch, examining their latest designs.

RECIPE

— · —

Birmingham Soup

The 1790s in England were a time of poor harvests and high food prices, and a number of soup kitchens were set up to provide cheap, nourishing food for those in need. One of those concerned about the plight of the poor was Matthew Boulton, of the Birmingham firm Boulton & Watt (see opposite). Birmingham Archives and Heritage Service holds an extensive collection of Matthew Boulton's papers, and in one of his notebooks, dated 1793, is his handwritten recipe for Birmingham Soup, to be sold at one penny a quart (2 pints, or 1.2 litres). This is a modern adaptation of Boulton's recipe. It is surprisingly good, rather like Scotch Broth, and makes a hearty broth for a cold winter's day.

    450g/1 lb lean stewing or braising beef, or shin of beef
    1.2 litres/2 pints water, or beef stock
    50g/2oz Quick Soup Mix (a mix of split peas, pearl barley, lentils and oatflakes that does not
        need to be soaked before using, available from supermarkets or health food shops)
    Alternatively, use 25g/1oz dried peas, soaked in water overnight, and 25g/1oz pearl barley,
        soaked in water for 2 hours, if preferred – as in the original recipe
    1 medium sized onion, peeled and chopped
    1 small turnip, peeled and diced into very small pieces
    1 large carrot, peeled and diced into very small pieces
    1 medium sized potato, peeled and diced into very small pieces
    2 tablespoonfuls medium oatmeal
    Salt and pepper to taste
    One slice of bread per person, with their crusts cut off
    Vegetable oil, or lard or dripping, for frying
    1 tablespoonful chopped fresh parsley to garnish

Trim the meat, and cut it into very small pieces. Put the meat into a large saucepan with the Quick Soup Mix (or the soaked pearl barley and dried peas), and cover with 1.2 litres (2 pints) of cold water, or beef stock. Bring it slowly to the boil, skimming off the scum as it rises. Add the prepared vegetables, bring back to the boil, then reduce to a low heat, cover the pan and leave to simmer gently for 2½ hours. Mix the oatmeal to a paste with a little water and add to the broth. Bring it to the boil again, then season with salt and pepper, reduce the heat and simmer, uncovered, for a further 20 minutes, stirring occasionally as the soup thickens, so it does not stick to the bottom of the pan. The original recipe ends: The Bread is cut in small pieces and put in when removed from the fire. The Bread is much better when fried in Lard or Dripping. When the soup is ready to serve, cut the bread slices into small cubes. Heat some oil or dripping in a frying pan and fry the bread cubes for a minute or so, until they are crisp and golden on both sides. Serve the soup in individual bowls with the fried bread cubes thrown on top and a little finely chopped fresh parsley scattered over them.

— · —

RECIPE

— · —

Brummie Bacon Cakes

These traditional snacks from Birmingham make a tasty and filling breakfast dish.

> 50g/2oz streaky bacon
> 225g/8oz self-raising flour
> Half a teaspoonful salt
> 25g/1oz butter or margarine
> 75g/3oz grated Cheddar cheese
> 150ml/ ¼ pint milk
> 1 tablespoonful tomato ketchup
> A dash of Worcestershire Sauce, to taste
> Milk for glazing

Pre-heat the oven to 200°C/400°F/Gas Mark 6.

Grill the bacon until crisp, and chop into small pieces. Sieve the flour and salt into a bowl and rub in the butter or margarine until the mixture resembles fine breadcrumbs. Add the chopped bacon and one third of the cheese.

Mix the milk, ketchup and Worcestershire Sauce together in a separate bowl. Add the dry ingredients, and mix together well to make a soft dough. Roll out on a floured board into a circle about 18-20cm (7-8 inches) in diameter.

Brush the top with milk and cut the dough into 8 wedges. Arrange them on a greased baking sheet and sprinkle with the remaining cheese. Bake in the pre-heated oven for about 30 minutes until crisp.

— · —

Birmingham, New Street 1890 B100001z

FISH

—.—

RECIPE

—.—

Severn Brown Trout

Rising 2000 ft (610 metres) above sea level upon the wild slopes of Plynlimon in Wales, the River Severn is the longest river in Britain, at 220 miles in length. It flows through both Shropshire and Worcestershire before reaching Gloucestershire and discharging into the Bristol Channel, and the county towns of Shrewsbury and Worcester stand on its banks. This is a traditional way from Worcestershire of serving trout. Serves 4, so increase the quantities for more.

> 4 cleaned trout, traditionally with head and tail left on
> Salt and freshly ground black pepper
> 150ml/ ¼ pint of cider
> A good squeeze of lemon juice
> 1 teaspoonful freshly chopped parsley in a cup of diluted
>   tarragon vinegar
> 25g/1oz butter, cut into small pieces

Pre-heat the oven to 180°C/350°F/Gas Mark 4.

Pat the trout dry and place in an ovenproof dish, tailed and headed if preferred. Add the seasoning, cider, lemon juice and parsley in vinegar. Cover the dish with its lid or foil, and bake in the pre-heated oven for 25 minutes.

Remove the dish from the oven and baste the fish with the liquid. Place small pieces of butter all over the fish and return the dish to the oven without its lid for another 7-10 minutes, so that the fish brown thoroughly.

—.—

RECIPE

Salmon with Cucumber Sauce

Both the River Severn and the River Wye, which flows through Herefordshire to meet the Severn estuary just below Chepstow, are famous for their trout and salmon. Salmon served with a cream and cucumber sauce is a traditional dish in many parts of England, and this is an ideal dish for hot summer days.

1.8kg/4 lbs salmon, gutted and scaled
A small amount of melted butter, for brushing on to the salmon
3 parsley or thyme sprigs
Half a lemon, cut into 2 further segments
1 large cucumber, peeled
25g/1oz butter
115ml/4 fl oz dry white wine
3 tablespoonfuls of finely chopped dill
4 tablespoonfuls of sour cream, or natural yogurt if preferred
Salt and pepper

Pre-heat the oven to 220°C/425°F/Gas Mark 7.

Season the salmon and brush it inside and out with melted butter. Place the herbs and lemon in the cavity. Wrap the salmon in foil, folding the edges together securely, then bake in the pre-heated oven for 15 minutes. Remove the fish from the oven and leave in the foil for 1 hour, then remove the skin from the salmon.

Meanwhile, halve the cucumber lengthways, scoop out the seeds, and dice the flesh. Place the cucumber in a colander, toss lightly with salt, leave for about 30 minutes to drain, then rinse well and pat dry.

Heat the butter in a small saucepan, add the cucumber and cook for about 2 minutes, until translucent but not soft. Add the wine to the pan and boil briskly until the cucumber is dry. Stir the dill and sour cream or yogurt into the cucumber. Season to taste and serve immediately with salmon.

RECIPE

—.—

Grilled Grayling

Grayling is a small freshwater fish that is similar to a brown trout, and can be found in the fast rivers and streams of Herefordshire. It has an excellent flavour, but does not keep very well after it is caught, so it should be eaten as soon as possible. Serves 4.

> 4 good-sized grayling
> 1 tablespoonful of fresh herbs such as chervil, chives, tarragon and parsley
> 115g/4oz butter
> Salt and pepper

Clean the fish thoroughly, and make two diagonal slits to the bone on both sides with a sharp knife. Chop the herbs finely and mix them with the butter, and season the mixture with salt and pepper. Smear half the herb butter on to the fish, making sure that it goes into the cuts. Pre-heat the grill, and grill the fish for 4 minutes, then turn the fish over, spread the other sides with the butter as before, and grill the other side for 4 minutes. Serve immediately, with the juices from the grill pan poured over the fish.

—.—

Ross-on-Wye, The River 1901 47887A

Cropthorne, The Mill and the Ferry 1910 62353x

MEAT, GAME AND POULTRY

In the past, in both the country towns and villages and the industrial towns of the West Midland counties of England, people made the best possible use of economical cuts of meat, and many traditional dishes evolved using offal, off-cuts and cheap parts of the animal. These dishes included cow heel jelly, pigs' trotters, chitterlings, tripe and onions (see page 19), haslet (a meat loaf that is eaten cold, cut into slices) and faggots, which were often called 'Poor Man's Goose' in many parts of England. Faggots are still very popular in the West Midlands. Homemade faggots are very nutritious, and the recipe on the opposite page is a modernised version that brings the dish up to date with a special gravy. If mincing up all the meat yourself does not appeal, ask your butcher to do it for you.

Shrewsbury, The Cattle Market 1891 28949

RECISE

~ . ~

Faggots with Onion and Red Wine Gravy

For the faggots:
25g/1oz unsalted butter
1 medium onion, peeled and finely chopped
175g/6oz minced pigs' liver
2 lambs' or pigs' hearts, trimmed and cut
   into chunks
450g/1 lb belly pork, trimmed and rind removed
Half a teaspoonful of ground mace
4 tablespoonfuls freshly chopped chives
1 teaspoonful freshly chopped sage leaves
1 egg, beaten
Salt and freshly ground pepper
115g/4oz fresh white breadcrumbs
25g/1oz beef dripping or 3 tablespoonfuls
   olive oil

For the gravy:
4 red onions, peeled, and with each onion
   cut into 8 wedges
4 sprigs of fresh thyme
1 tablespoonful olive oil
900ml/1½ pints fresh beef stock
300ml/ ½ pint red wine
Salt and freshly ground black pepper

Melt the butter in a small saucepan and add the chopped onion. Cook until soft and transparent, then leave to cool slightly. Place the belly pork onto a chopping board and cut into portions. Place the minced liver into a large glass bowl and place under the blade of a mincer. Using a fine blade of a mincer, mince the pork belly and hearts directly into the bowl with the liver. Add the cooled chopped onion, mace, chives, sage, beaten egg and salt and pepper. Stir in the breadcrumbs. Using your hands, shape the mixture into 12 patties. Place them on a plate and chill in the fridge for about 1 hour.

Pre-heat the oven to 200°C/400°F/Gas Mark 6, then place the red onion wedges into a large roasting pan or ovenproof dish. Add the thyme and drizzle over the olive oil. Place in the oven and roast uncovered for 40 minutes until the onions are caramelised. Meanwhile heat the dripping or olive oil in a large frying pan. Fry the faggots until golden brown on both sides. Place the stock and wine in a small saucepan, bring to the boil and reduce by a third. Remove the roasted onions from the oven and lay the faggots on top. Pour over the gravy liqueur. Reduce the oven temperature to 180°C/350°F/Gas Mark 4 and cook the faggots in the oven for 40 minutes. Place two to three faggots onto a plate. Top with a spoonful of the onions and pour over the gravy. Serve the faggots with mashed potatoes and green vegetables, particularly peas, which are the traditional accompaniment to faggots.

~ . ~

A Taste of THE WEST MIDLANDS

A dish that was traditionally very popular all over the West Midlands region of England in former times was tripe and onions. Many people nowadays are averse to the thought of eating tripe, but tripe was commonly eaten in the past and for those who like it, it is a very good dish, succulent in texture. Tripe is the edible stomach linings of an ox or cow. The first lining is called 'blanket', the second 'honeycomb' and the third 'double' or 'thick seam'. The appearance of the three linings is different, but they all taste the same. There are a number of traditional methods of preparing tripe, but one of the favourite methods is that given on the opposite page, plain and simple, with the tripe slow-cooked with onions for several hours, simmered in milk which is then used to make a rich creamy sauce to accompany it.

Coventry, Butcher's Row 1892 30916A

RECIPE

— . —

Tripe and Onions

Tripe is not often found in supermarkets, so you will probably need to get the tripe from a traditional butcher, if you are lucky enough to still have one in your area. Ask for a mixture of all the different parts of tripe for this dish. This amount is enough for 4 people.

450g/1 lb best prepared and dressed tripe, washed
3 large onions, peeled and sliced
550ml/1 pint milk
25g/1oz butter
25g/1oz plain flour
1 bay leaf
A pinch of freshly grated nutmeg
1 level teaspoonful of dry mustard powder
Salt and freshly ground black pepper
1 rounded tablespoonful of finely chopped fresh parsley

Place the tripe in a saucepan and cover with lightly salted cold water. Bring to the boil, then remove from the heat, drain the tripe and rinse it under cold running water. Cut the tripe into 2.5cm (1 inch) pieces. Put a layer of the onions in the rinsed-out pan, then the tripe, then the rest of the onions. Pour in the milk, and add the bayleaf, the freshly grated nutmeg and just a pinch of salt. Put the pan on a medium heat and bring the milk very slowly to just below the boil, then reduce the heat to very low, cover the pan with its lid and leave to simmer gently for as long as possible, until the tripe is very tender – at least 2 hours, longer if you can. Stir occasionally to prevent any sticking. When the tripe is ready, remove the pan from the heat and strain it, reserving the cooking liquid. Measure the liquid, and make it up to 550ml (1 pint) with more milk if necessary. Keep the tripe and onions warm whilst you make the sauce. Melt the butter in a saucepan, stir in the flour and the mustard powder, and allow it to cook gently for 2-3 minutes, stirring, then gradually blend in the tripe cooking liquid, a little at a time, stirring constantly as you bring the sauce to the boil and it thickens. Reduce the heat and add the tripe and onions to the sauce, then simmer the mixture for 10 minutes, without allowing it to boil. Turn out the tripe and onions into a warmed serving bowl and garnish with finely chopped fresh parsley. Serve immediately, piping hot, with potatoes and seasonal vegetables.

— . —

Stourbridge, High Street 1931 84685

The Black Country

In 1974 a 'new' county called West Midlands was created, which comprised parts of Staffordshire, Worcestershire and Warwickshire, including Birmingham and other places formerly in Warwickshire such as Sutton Coldfield, Solihull and Coventry. Part of what is now the 'new' county of West Midlands is the Black Country, an area taken from parts of Staffordshire and Worcestershire. A common definition of the Black Country encompasses most of the Metropolitan Boroughs of Dudley, Sandwell, Walsall and the City of Wolverhampton. An alternative geological definition follows the outcroppings of the South Staffordshire 'thick' coal seam, and on this definition the outcropping of the coal seams near Halesowen and Stourbridge provides a southern boundary. Within this definition, parts of Walsall, Wolverhampton and Stourbridge are not within the Black Country, but West Bromwich is. The name 'Black Country' probably derived from the smoke and dirt of what was for many centuries an area of heavy industrialisation. Descriptions of this region in the 17th and 18th centuries often describe scenes of a 'hell on earth', and Thomas Carlyle (1795-1881) wrote of 'a frightful scene (with) a dense cloud of pestilential smoke (where) the whole region burns like a volcano spitting fire from a thousand tubes of brick'. Dudley is traditionally seen as the capital of the Black Country. Exploitation of Dudley's natural resources began well before the Industrial Revolution and the town centre became the site of many industries, most of which were in the Black Country tradition of 'metal bashing', notably that of fender and fire-iron manufacture.

For many years the name 'Black Country' was almost a term of disparagement, describing a hardworking but unattractive area, but in recent times the growth of the tourist industry has turned it into a powerful marketing tool that is used and borne with pride. The region's industrial past has now become something of great interest, and the superb Black Country Living Museum in Dudley is a popular visitor attraction. Another way in which Dudley celebrates its proud industrial heritage is with the sculptured frieze in the town centre, seen in the photograph on the opposite page. Installed in 1963, it depicts, at each end, the area's traditional industries of chain-making and coal-mining, with a mother and child in the centre representing education.

RECIPE

Black Country Beef Stew

450g/1 lb stewing steak
300ml/ ½ pint mild ale
300ml/ ½ pint beef stock
225g/8oz black pudding, sliced
115g/4oz mushrooms
2 large onions
1 tablespoonful tomato purée
1 teaspoonful parsley, finely chopped
Half a teaspoonful sage, finely chopped
Half a teaspoonful thyme, finely chopped
1 bay leaf
Salt and pepper
Oil for frying

Slice the onions and dice the steak. Heat a little oil in a medium-sized saucepan and fry the onions until softened. Add the diced steak a few pieces at a time and lightly brown. Add the ale, tomato purée and the chopped fresh herbs and the bay leaf, and season to taste. Simmer gently for 20 minutes to reduce slightly, then add the stock and simmer for 1½ hours. Fry the slices of black pudding and mushrooms, and add to the stew. Return the stew to the boil briefly, then serve with new potatoes and green vegetables.

Dudley, The Sculpture Frieze, Birdcage Walk c1965 D103123

23

Wolverhampton, Queen Street c1900 W285001

RECIPE

—·—

Grey Peas and Bacon

Grey Peas and Bacon is a dish from the Black Country that was often eaten on Bonfire Night. The proper peas to use are dried maple peas, also known as field peas or pigeon peas – they are often used as pigeon food, and can be bought from pet food suppliers if they prove hard to find. Maple peas are brown, but go grey when they are cooked, hence their name of 'grey peas'. If you can't find maple peas you can use black-eyed peas, dried green peas or even dried yellow split peas instead. Adding bicarbonate of soda to the water during the soaking process helps the peas to soften when they are cooked, but you can omit this if you prefer. Some people like to make this with just the peas and bacon, omitting the onion and pearl barley. The longer you leave this to cook, the better – the old Black Country tradition was 'soak for a day – cook for a day'!

450g/1 lb dried grey peas (or alternative, if they are hard to find – see above)
450g/1 lb bacon, chopped into small pieces
1 large onion, peeled and finely chopped
3oz/75g pearl barley
Plenty of water for soaking the peas and barley
600ml/1 pint water or stock
Oil for frying
Pepper (you should not need to add salt, as the bacon will make the dish salty)
1 teaspoonful bicarbonate of soda

Wash the peas, put them in a large bowl, add the pearl barley and the bicarbonate of soda (if using), then put in enough water to cover them plus some on top, and leave to soak overnight. Next day, drain the peas and barley and rinse well. Heat a little oil in a large pan and fry the bacon pieces until browned and crispy. Add 600ml (1 pint) of water or stock, bring to the boil and add the soaked peas and barley and the chopped onion. Bring back to the boil and boil hard for 10 minutes, then cover the pan, reduce the heat to low and leave to simmer gently for at least 3 hours, longer if you can, topping up the pan now and again with more boiling water as necessary, until the peas are tender. Add a little salt to taste if necessary in the last half an hour of cooking. Serve with crusty bread.

—·—

RECIPE

—.—

Groaty Pudding

One of the most popular vegetables found in gardens and allotments in the West Midlands is the leek. A highlight for vegetable growers in the area is the Annual Horticultural and Midland Leek Show which is part of the Sandwell Community Show held every August in Sandwell, a metropolitan borough made up of the towns of Oldbury, Rowley Regis, Smethwick, Tipton, Wednesbury, Cradley Heath, Tividale and West Bromwich. The Midland Leek Show attracts competitors from throughout the region, and gives growers the chance to win much-coveted prizes for their giant vegetables. However, for cooking purposes it is better to use smaller leeks! Leeks are one of the ingredients of Groaty Pudding (or Groaty Dick), a traditional dish from the Black Country that was often served on Bonfire Night. Groats are whole grains of oats with the husks removed, but before they have been ground to produce oatmeal, or rolled to make rolled oats; they are not the same thing as jumbo whole rolled oats that you can buy for making porridge. If groats prove hard to find, they can be bought over the internet, or try looking in health food shops or even pet food suppliers – they are often sold as bird food.

> 450g/1 lb stewing beef or shin of beef
> 2 onions, peeled and finely chopped
> 2 leeks, trimmed, washed and finely sliced
> 225g/8oz oat groats
> 1 bayleaf
> Salt and pepper to taste
> Enough boiling water or hot beef stock to cover ingredients in cooking pot

Pre-heat the oven to 150°C/300°F/Gas Mark 2. Trim the meat and cut it into bite-sized pieces. Put the meat, the prepared onions and leeks and the bayleaf into a large ovenproof dish (preferably an earthenware one). Season to taste with salt and pepper. Pour in enough boiling water or hot beef stock to cover the ingredients. Cover the dish with its lid and cook in the pre-heated oven for at least 3 hours, or longer if you can. The groats will absorb the cooking liquid and expand, thickening the stew. Serve with potatoes, or crusty bread if preferred – in the past, Groaty Pudding was often served spread on slices of bread.

—.—

RECIPE

—ㆍ—

Warwickshire Stew

This traditional dish from Warwickshire is a way of cooking the cheaper but tougher beef cuts gently and slowly.

675g/1½ lbs stewing steak

2 tablespoonfuls seasoned plain flour

1 tablespoonful oil or beef dripping

150ml/ ¼ pint beef stock or red wine

6 potatoes, diced

4 carrots, diced

2 onions, cut into quarters

350g/12oz tomatoes

115g/4oz mushrooms,
   cut into quarters

2 cloves of garlic, crushed

1 tablespoonful chopped parsley

Salt and pepper

Pre-heat the oven to 140°C/275°F/Gas Mark 1. Cut the beef into cubes, and lightly dust with seasoned flour. Heat the oil in a frying pan and fry the beef cubes in batches, to seal and colour the meat. Remove the meat from the pan and place in a casserole dish, then add the stock or wine to the frying pan and heat gently, stirring all the time and making sure to scrape the bottom of the pan to collect all the flour. Add all the remaining ingredients to the casserole dish and pour over the warmed stock or wine. Cover and cook for about 5-6 hours.

—ㆍ—

Bidford-on-Avon, Broom
1910 62647

RECITE

~ • ~

Stuffed Chine of Pork

In Warwickshire in the past, a chine of pork stuffed with parsley was the traditional fare for Mothering Sunday. The chine is a cut from the back of the pig – if you can't get this, use a loin of pork joint instead.

> 1.5kg/3 lbs chine or loin of pork
> A good bunch of fresh parsley sprigs
> 1 egg yolk
> 175g/6oz fresh breadcrumbs
> 25g/1oz melted lard or butter

Pre-heat the oven to 220°C/425°F/Gas Mark 7. Boil the chine or loin for 30 minutes in a saucepan of water. Drain the meat and make several cuts into the lean part of the meat, about 1 inch/2.5cm apart. Stuff each incision with sprigs of parsley, stalk ends first. Brush the chine with the egg yolk and then coat it with the breadcrumbs, pressing them on firmly. Baste carefully with the melted lard or butter and roast in the pre-heated hot oven for 20 minutes, then reduce the heat to 180°C/350°F/Gas Mark 4 and cook for a further 20 minutes per pound/450g weight of meat, plus 20 minutes over.

~ • ~

Whitnash, The Village 1892 30990

A Taste of THE WEST MIDLANDS

Stratford-upon-Avon in Warwickshire is famous for its association with William Shakespeare, who was born in a house in Henley Street in 1564. In 1597 William Shakespeare purchased a house in Church Street in Stratford, known as New Place. He retired there at the end of his playwriting career, and it was where he died in 1616, on his 52nd birthday, of a fever which was said at the time to have been the result of a 'merry meeting' with his fellow poets Ben Jonson and Michael Drayton, at which they all drank too much. New Place was demolished in 1759, but the site of the house forms part of the garden beside the splendid timber-framed Nash's House, which houses the town museum. After his death Shakespeare left New Place to his eldest daughter Susanna. According to local tradition, in 1643, during the Civil War, Charles I's queen Henrietta Maria lodged there for three days as Susanna's guest on her way to Oxford with money, arms and ammunition for the king. Queen Henrietta Maria's stay was the first recorded royal visit in the history of Stratford, and was the cause of much celebration. The accounts of the borough chamberlain for the visit still survive, and under 'moneyes disbursed and payd' are a number of entries, including £3 18s 6d paid to 'Butchers for meate', 12s 6d to John Copland for 'Bread, cheese and Beare', and 5s 4d for '3 heens, I Coke, 8 chikins'. In total, the royal visit cost the borough the sum of £28 2s 11d.

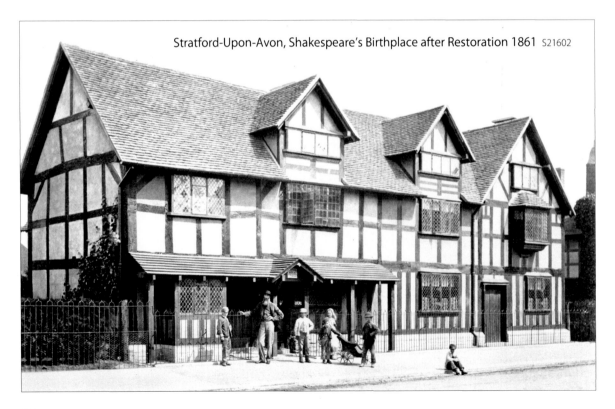

Stratford-Upon-Avon, Shakespeare's Birthplace after Restoration 1861 S21602

RECIPE

—·—

Savoury Sausage Pie

This recipe comes from Worcestershire. The filling for the pie was originally made from minced-up pieces of leftover pork after a pig was killed on the farm and the carcass had been butchered. It was often known as 'Bits and Pieces'.

> 350g/12oz shortcrust pastry
> 450g/1 lb pork sausagemeat
> 115g/4oz bacon bits, pork off-cuts or streaky bacon
> 1 cooking apple
> 1 tablespoonful chopped fresh parsley
> 2 beaten eggs
> 2 hard-boiled eggs, cut into quarters
> Salt and pepper

Pre-heat the oven to 190°C/375°F/Gas Mark 5.

Roll out the pastry on a lightly-floured surface, and use it to line a pie dish or flan tin, reserving enough pastry to make a lid.

Mash up the sausagemeat in a large bowl. Mince the bacon or pork. Grate the apple. Reserve a small amount of the beaten egg to glaze the pastry, then mix together all the filling ingredients, seasoning to taste. Place the filling in the pastry-lined pie dish or tin and add the pieces of hard-boiled eggs, pressing them in and covering them with the filling.

Roll out the remaining pastry to make a lid, moistening the pastry edges and pressing them well together to seal. Use the pastry trimmings to decorate the lid, if liked. Prick holes in the pastry lid with a fork to allow steam to escape, then brush the pastry with the reserved beaten egg mixed with a dessertspoonful of milk, to glaze.

Bake for 30 minutes in the pre-heated oven, then reduce the oven temperature to 180°C/350°F/Gas Mark 4 and cook for a further 15 minutes.

—·—

RECIPE

—·—

Evesham Chicken

This is another recipe from Worcestershire, this time combining chicken with apples from the Vale of Evesham, an area famous for its fruit and vegetables.

4 chicken pieces
25g/1oz seasoned flour
50g/2oz butter
1 onion, peeled and chopped
2 red-skinned eating apples, cored and cut into slices
450ml/ ¾ pint dry cider
2 teaspoonfuls mixed herbs
Salt and pepper
150ml/ ¼ pint single cream
1 tablespoonful chopped parsley, to garnish

Pre-heat the oven to 190°C/375°F/Gas Mark 5.

Toss the chicken pieces in the seasoned flour so that all sides are covered. Melt the butter in a large frying pan and fry the chicken pieces until all sides are lightly browned, then remove them to a casserole dish. Fry the chopped onion and sliced apples in the remaining fat in the pan until they are softened and golden, then add them to the casserole dish. Add any remaining seasoned flour to the fat in the pan, stir it in and cook gently for 2-3 minutes. Gradually add the cider, a little at a time, stirring continually so that no lumps are formed. Add the mixed herbs and season to taste.

Remove the pan from the heat and stir in the cream, then pour the sauce into the casserole dish. Cover and cook in the pre-heated oven for 1-1¼ hours. Serve garnished with chopped parsley.

—·—

Evesham, Bridge Street 1892 31106

RECIPE

— . —

Beef Olives

Herefordshire is famous for the quality of the beef that is reared in the county.

675g/1½ lbs topside of beef, cut into 8 thin strips
25g/1oz butter or margarine
2 slices of bacon, finely chopped
115g/4oz mushrooms, chopped
1 tablespoonful finely chopped parsley
Grated rind and juice of 1 lemon
115g/4oz fresh breadcrumbs
3 tablespoonfuls plain flour
3 tablespoonfuls oil
2 onions, sliced
450ml/ ¾ pint good brown stock
Salt and pepper

Pre-heat the oven to 160°C/325°F/Gas Mark 3.

Heat the butter or margarine, add the bacon and mushrooms and fry for about 3 minutes, then mix them with the parsley, lemon rind and juice, breadcrumbs and seasoning. Spread an equal amount of the breadcrumb mixture evenly over the beef slices, leaving a narrow border clear around the edge. Roll up the slices and tie securely with fine string, then dip the beef rolls in the flour to coat them lightly.

Heat the oil in a heavy shallow pan, then fry the beef rolls until lightly browned. Remove the beef rolls from the pan and keep warm. Add the onions to the pan and fry until browned. Stir in the remaining flour and cook until lightly browned. Gradually pour in the stock, stirring constantly, then bring to the boil, stirring, and simmer for 2-3 minutes.

Transfer the beef rolls to a casserole dish, pour over the sauce, then cover the casserole dish tightly and cook in the oven for 2 hours. When cooked, lift out the 'olives' and remove the string, then return them to the sauce and serve hot, garnished with chopped parsley.

— . —

Leominster, A Cottage in Vicarage Street 1906
55492x

RECIPE

Hereford Sausages

450g/1 lb good quality sausages

25g/1oz lard (or oil, for frying)

2 onions, peeled and finely chopped

2 rashers back bacon, cut into strips

1 heaped teaspoonful plain flour

3 tablespoonfuls dry cider, made up to 300ml (½ pint) with vegetable
  or ham stock

1 bay leaf

Salt and pepper

115g/4oz mushrooms, sliced

Fry the sausages in the lard or oil for about 20 minutes, until they are browned on all sides. Remove the sausages from the pan, and pour away some of the fat. Add the chopped onions and bacon to the remaining fat in the pan and cook gently for 5 minutes. Sprinkle on the flour and cook for 2-3 minutes, stirring well. Gradually add the cider and stock, a little at a time, stirring continually, and bring to the boil. Add the bay leaf and sausages and season to taste. Reduce the heat, cover the pan with its lid and simmer for 20 minutes. Add the sliced mushrooms for the last 10 minutes of the simmering time. Remove the bay leaf when ready to serve.

Hereford, Old House
1898 41752

RECIPE

—·—

Shropshire Fidget Pie

This recipe from Shropshire is a hearty and flavoursome pie that was traditionally made at harvest time, either to feed the harvesters working in the fields or to welcome them home when they had finished their day's work – the key ingredients of apples and onions are fresh and plentiful at this time of the year. One theory for the unusual name is that 'fitched' meant five-sided, and the pies may originally have been made in a five-sided shape. However, another interpretation is that 'fitchett' was an old name for a pole-cat; as polecats are known for their strong smell, the name may originally have been a light-hearted comment on the strong aroma that filled the kitchen as these pies were cooking. However, they taste delicious! This pie can be eaten either hot or cold.

225g/8oz shortcrust pastry
4 medium-sized potatoes, peeled and cut into thin slices
3 onions, sliced
3 cooking apples, peeled, cored and sliced
50g/2oz butter
3 rashers of sweetcure gammon, with the rinds cut off, and cut into strips
1 tablespoonful brown sugar
Salt and freshly ground black pepper
300ml/ ½ pint vegetable stock
Milk or a beaten egg, to glaze the pastry

Pre-heat the oven to 200°C/400°F/Gas Mark 6. Melt the butter in a large pan and lightly fry the sliced potatoes, onions and apples until they are softening and golden. Remove from the pan with a slotted spoon and keep hot. Lightly fry the gammon pieces in the pan in the remaining fat. Place layers of the gammon, potatoes, onions and apples in a large pie dish, seasoning to taste with the salt, pepper and sugar as you go. When all the ingredients have been used, pour on the stock. Roll out the pastry on a lightly-floured surface and use it to make a lid to cover the pie. Cut a hole in the centre of the lid for steam to escape – a pie funnel can also be used if liked. Press down the edges of the pastry well to the rim of the dish to seal. Decorate the pie lid with the pastry trimmings, and brush with milk or beaten egg to glaze. Bake in the pre-heated hot oven for 30 minutes, then reduce the oven temperature to 160°C/325°F/Gas Mark 3 and bake for a further 20-30 minutes, until the pastry is crisp and golden brown.

—·—

All Stretton, The Long Mynd Hills, Collecting Wood 1910 62742

RECICE

—·—

Staffordshire Rabbit Pie with Forcemeat Balls

225g/8oz shortcrust pastry
1 rabbit, jointed
Salt and pepper
1 bay leaf
1 bouquet garni
A little milk to glaze the pastry

For the forcemeat balls:
175g/6oz fresh breadcrumbs
75g/3oz butter or shredded suet
A pinch of thyme
A pinch of chopped parsley
Salt and pepper
Juice of 1 lemon
1 egg, beaten

Place the rabbit joints in a bowl and cover with cold salted water. Leave to soak for half an hour, then place the joints in a large pan with 600ml (1 pint) of fresh water, salt, pepper, the bay leaf and the bouquet garni. Bring to the boil, then reduce the heat, cover the pan and leave to simmer for 1 hour. While the rabbit is simmering, make the forcemeat balls: mix the breadcrumbs with the butter or shredded suet, add the thyme, parsley and seasoning and mix well together. Make the mixture into a stiff paste with the lemon juice and beaten egg, then form into small balls by rolling it in your hands. Drop the forcemeat balls into the pan in which the rabbit is cooking, and simmer very gently for a further half an hour.

Pre-heat the oven to 200°C/400°F/Gas Mark 6.

When the forcemeat balls are cooked, place the rabbit joints in a pie dish with the forcemeat balls on top, and pour in about 300ml/ ½ pint of the cooking liquid. Roll out the pastry on a lightly-floured surface and use it to make a lid for the pie, pressing the edges firmly to the rim of the dish to seal. Brush the pastry with a little milk to glaze, then bake in the pre-heated oven for about 30 minutes, until the pastry is crisp and golden brown.

—·—

Tamworth, The Town Hall c1950 T157001

Birmingham, Paradise Street and the Town Hall 1896 37274

The Balti Triangle

Present-day Birmingham is a vibrant, multi-cultural city and is renowned for its wide range of excellent restaurants serving cuisine from all over the world. It is especially famous for its superb Asian restaurants, particularly its balti restaurants in the so-called 'Balti Triangle' of the Sparkbrook, Balsall Heath and Ladypool areas of the city.

A balti is a spicy aromatic dish originally devised in the Sparkbrook area of Birmingham in the 1970s by residents from the Pakistani Kashmiri community who were unhappy with the oily food available in the area at the time. It is cooked in a special flat-bottomed two-handled cooking pot made of thin steel, which heats up quickly when placed over a flame and allows food to be cooked very swiftly using the stir-fry process, which retains the goodness and flavour of the food and spices whilst using very little oil. The food is both cooked and served to the table in the cooking pot, also called a 'balti', and thus the name of the cooking utensil has also become the name of the dish that is cooked in it. A true balti cooked in a proper balti pan is made with meat and vegetables such as tomatoes, onions, ginger and garlic, and authentic, best quality, freshly ground spices, combined with herbs like coriander, fenugreek and mint. A good balti has a distinctive fresh flavour, where the dish is not overpowered by heat or spice. A well-prepared authentic balti is a work of art and a definite gastronomic experience. A balti is traditionally not served with rice but with large naan bread pieces.

Many Asian restaurants around the country claim to make and serve the dish, but you only get an authentic balti in Birmingham. In recent years members of Birmingham City Council have considered applying for the balti to be given PGI (Protected Geographical Indication) and PDO (Protected Destination of Origin) status, to ensure that only dishes made in Birmingham can carry the name. Supporters of the proposal say the balti was created in one particular area by members of a specific community at a particular time, and the inferior concoctions served in curry houses elsewhere are nothing like a good Birmingham balti. If it doesn't come from Brum, then it isn't a true balti!

VEGETABLE AND CHEESE DISHES

The Birmingham Onion Fair

Despite the modern development that has taken place in Birmingham, the Bull Ring is still the centre of the city. It used to be the venue for an important annual event, the famous Birmingham Onion Fair, which celebrated the onion harvest in the autumn. This account of the Fair appeared in 'The Illustrated London News' in October 1872:

'The greatest manufacturing town of the Midland shires has retained a considerable trade in the agricultural produce of the surrounding country···But the unique feature of this particular aspect of Birmingham, as an agricultural market, is the Michaelmas Onion Fair. It is held on the last Thursday in September, in the wide open place called the Bull Ring, which is situated in the centre of town, in front of St. Martin's Church. This growth of this savoury vegetable is the object of much attention by many of the neighbouring market-gardeners and farmers, who find the soil and climate well adapted to its cultivation. Nowhere can such large quantities be seen or of finer quality, than in the special Fair at Birmingham, which took place as usual on Thursday week. The onions are piled in stacks, heaped in wooden crates or wicker baskets, spread upon wide stalls, or suspended in perpendicular ropes from cross-poles overhead, in the variety of arrangement for effective display. The air is fully charged with their pungent odour, causing the unaccustomed eye, perhaps, to shed an involuntary tear, while engaged in the inspection of their diverse kinds, though not a sorry sight. The dealers and customers at this Fair are mostly the country folk of Warwickshire, with a few tradesmen of the town and some of the workmen's wives for the onion gives a palatable relish to a poor man's dinner or supper.'

The sale of onions at the Fair in the past was accompanied by stalls, sideshows and amusements, and special excursion trains were run to the event from all over the area. However, after 1875 the onions and the amusements side of the Fair parted company. The amusements went to Aston and developed into a modern funfair, whilst the once-famous Onion Fair in the city centre for the sale of 'the savoury vegetable' is now just a part of Birmingham's history.

Here are two onion recipes recalling the importance of this vegetable to Birmingham in the past, when it was sold in huge quantities at the city's famous Onion Fair (see page 45). One recipe is for a traditional onion gravy, the other is for onion bhajis, linking Birmingham's past with its multi-cultural population of present times, and celebrating the modern city's reputation as a centre of Asian cuisine. Onion bhajis are savoury Asian snacks that have become popular all over Britain. They are small patties or balls made of sliced onions and flour, flavoured with spices and deep fried. There are many recipe variations, but they are very easy to make. They should properly be made with chick pea or gram flour which is available from Asian food stores, but if this is hard to find you can use plain flour instead. They can be eaten either as a snack on their own, or as a starter or side dish to a curry – try serving them with mango chutney or with a cucumber and mint raita (made by adding finely chopped cucumber and fresh mint leaves to natural yogurt).

RECIPE

~ . ~

Onion Gravy

Onion gravy is a traditional delicacy that is still popular, and is particularly good served with sausages, especially those made from traditional pig breeds like the Tamworth which originated from Staffordshire.

> 2 tablespoonfuls vegetable oil
> 1 large onion, halved then sliced
> 1 tablespoonful plain flour
> 360ml/12fl oz chicken stock
> 1 teaspoonful chopped mixed herbs, fresh or dried
> 1 teaspoonful Worcestershire Sauce

Heat the oil in a medium sized saucepan. Add the onions and sauté for about 10 minutes, until brown. Sprinkle the flour over the onions and continue to cook, stirring gently, for 2-3 minutes. Gradually add the stock, herbs and Worcestershire Sauce and continue to cook until thickened, stirring all the time. Partially cover and cook for a further 10-15 minutes to allow the flavours to develop, stirring from time to time.

~ . ~

RECIPE

—·—

Onion Bhajis (Onion Bhajias)

Onion bhajis should be mildly spicy, not hot, but increase the amounts of spices in this recipe if you prefer their flavour to be more prominent. This amount makes about 16 small onion bhajis, or about 8 larger ones.

115g/4oz chick pea flour or gram flour (or use plain flour instead, if this is hard to find)
1 teaspoonful Garam Masala, or curry powder
Half a teaspoonful chilli powder
Half a teaspoonful ground turmeric
Half a teaspoonful ground cumin
Half a teaspoonful baking powder
Salt to taste
1 large onion or 2 medium onions, peeled, cut into halves and then finely
    sliced into long thin strands
1 green chilli, deseeded and finely chopped
1 tablespoonful mango chutney
1 heaped tablespoonful finely chopped fresh coriander leaves
A small amount of cold water, for mixing
Vegetable oil, for deep frying

Sift the flour, Garam Masala or curry powder, chilli powder, turmeric, cumin, baking powder and salt into a large mixing bowl. Add the onion slices, chopped chilli, mango chutney and chopped coriander leaves, and mix it all together well. Gradually add a little water to the flour mixture, just enough to combine it all together in a thick, stiff paste, and mix it until the onions are well coated. The mixture should not be runny, but should stick and hold together well. Leave the mixture to stand for 10 minutes for the flavours to develop. Heat the oil in a large pan or deep fat fryer to 180°C/350°F, or until a cube of bread browns quickly in it. When it is ready, drop spoonfuls of the mixture into the hot fat – about the size of an egg or a golf ball for small bhajis, or the size of a tennis ball for larger ones. Fry the bhajis in the hot oil in batches until they are crisp and golden brown on both sides; this should take about 3 minutes on each side for small bhajis, but longer for larger ones. Allow the oil to heat up again between each batch. Remove from the oil with a slotted spoon and drain well on kitchen paper. Either eat them straight away, hot and crisp, or store in an airtight container and eat cold. They can also be reheated in the oven to crisp them up and serve hot when needed.

—·—

RECIPE

—.—

Cheese, Onion and Potato Pie

At the south of the borough of Solihull is the small village of Earlswood, which straddles the county border of Warwickshire and West Midlands. Earlswood is the home of Fowlers of Earlswood, the oldest family cheese-making firm in the country. Their range of traditional handcrafted cheeses can be found in supermarkets and Fowlers are also regular stallholders at the Birmingham City Centre Farmers Market, held on the first and third Wednesdays of each month in New Street. Their range includes cheeses flavoured with garlic and parsley, chilli, sage, cracked black pepper, onion and chives, and real ale and mustard. Why not use your own favourite Fowlers cheese in this savoury pie.

225g/8oz potatoes
75g/3oz hard cheese of choice, grated
1 small onion, very finely chopped
25g/1oz butter or margarine
Salt and pepper
80ml/3fl oz milk
1 dessertspoonful chopped fresh parsley

Boil the potatoes until they soften. Melt half the butter or margarine in a pan and fry the chopped onion until it is soft and golden. Drain the cooked potatoes. Add the milk and remaining butter or margarine to the potatoes, season to taste and mash well until smooth.
Add the cooked onion, all but 2 tablespoonfuls of the grated cheese and the parsley to the mashed potatoes and mix it all together well. Put the mixture into a warmed shallow ovenproof dish, and smooth the top. Sprinkle the rest of the melted cheese on top, and brown under a hot grill before serving.

As a variation to this recipe, before sprinkling the cheese on the top of the pie, make four hollows on the top of the pie (by pressing the back of a spoon into the topping), and drop an egg into each hollow, topped with a small dot of butter. Sprinkle the grated cheese between the eggs, and bake in the pre-heated oven at 190°C/375°F/Gas Mark 5 for about 15-20 minutes, until the eggs have set.

—.—

RECIPE

—·—

Worcestershire Supper Savoury

One of Worcester's most famous products is a condiment that originated in India. Its recipe was brought to England by Lord Sandys after a tour of duty in the sub-continent, and two chemists, William Perrins and John Wheely Lea, tried to recreate its flavour, at first unsuccessfully. However, the concoction that we now know as Worcestershire Sauce improved greatly after long maturation, and Mr Lea and Mr Perrins started to sell it successfully from their premises in Broad Street in the city.

4 thick slices of bread
4 slices of cheese
Mustard to taste
Worcestershire sauce
Salt
4 tomatoes
4 slices of bacon

This serves 4, so increase the amounts for more people. Pre-heat the oven to 200°C/400°F/Gas Mark 6. Put a slice of cheese on each piece of bread, and spread with a little mustard. Sprinkle a dash of Worcestershire sauce over each slice, and add salt to taste. Slice the tomatoes and arrange on top of each slice, then lay a slice of bacon on top. Place on a hot baking tray and bake in the pre-heated oven for about 15-20 minutes, until the bacon is cooked and crisp.

—·—

Worcester
Broad Street 1908
59641

Worcester, The River Severn from the Cathedral Tower c1960 W141077

PUDDINGS, PIES AND DESSERTS

— . —

RECIPE

— . —

Pears in Spiced Red Wine

Pears are believed to have been a Worcestershire symbol since at least 1415, when the banner of the men of Worcestershire in Henry V's army was said to show 'a pear tree laden with fruit'. The town of Pershore was once so famous for its pear trees that the fruit gave its name to the town – 'Pershore' was contracted from the town's original name of Pearshore, and the city of Worcester's coat of arms consists of a castle and three black pears. The species of black pear on Worcester's coat of arms is quite unpalatable in its raw state, and slow cooking in red wine is recommended – but any type of pears can be used in this dessert recipe, black or otherwise.

6 large, firm pears
300-450ml/ ½ - ¾ pint red wine
25g/1oz brown sugar
A pinch of ground cinnamon
A pinch of ground ginger

Pre-heat the oven to 180°C/350°F/Gas Mark 4.

Peel the pears, and stand them in a deep ovenproof dish. Mix the red wine with the brown sugar and spices, and pour it over the pears. Bake in the pre-heated oven for 20-30 minutes, until the pears are tender. Serve with some of the liquid spooned over each pear.

— . —

RECIPE

—·—

Plum Charlotte

The area around Pershore in the Vale of Evesham in Worcestershire is also famous as a centre of English plum production. Victoria plums are the most popular nowadays, but plums in traditional local varieties are still grown here, such as 'Pershore Purple' and 'Pershore Yellow Egg'.

450g/1 lb plums
Enough slices of bread, white or brown to line a pie dish
  – stale bread is ideal for this recipe
50g/2oz butter
115g/4oz demerara sugar

Pre-heat the oven to 180°C/350°F/Gas Mark 4.

Grease a shallow 600ml (1 pint) pie dish. Wash the plums, cut them in half and remove the stones. Butter the slices of bread, and use most of them to line the bottom and sides of the pie dish, buttered side down, reserving a few slices for to use as a 'lid'. Sprinkle a little of the sugar over the bread slices. Cover the slices with a layer of plums, cut side up, and sprinkle the plums with a little sugar. Continue to add layers of plums and sugar until all the plums have been used. Cover the top with the remaining bread slices, buttered side up. Bake in the pre-heated oven for 20-30 minutes. This can be served hot or cold, with cream or custard.

—·—

RECITE

—·—

Evesham Apple Pie

Here is another recipe from the Vale of Evesham, the famous fruit-growing region of England that is particularly known for its apples and plums.

225g/8oz shortcrust pastry, with 2 teaspoonfuls of caster sugar and ¼ teaspoonful of ground cinnamon added to the flour when making the pastry

1kg/2 lbs cooking apples

2 tablespoonfuls orange marmalade

Half a teaspoonful ground cinnamon

25g/1oz butter

75g/3oz brown sugar

A little caster sugar to finish

Roll out two thirds of the pastry on a lightly-floured surface, and use it to line a greased pie or flan tin. Place in the fridge to rest, together with the reserved pastry.

Peel, core and slice the apples and stew them in a small amount of water until they are soft and pulpy. Remove the pan from the heat and stir in the orange marmalade, ground cinnamon, brown sugar and butter. Mix well until the butter has melted, then leave to cool.

Pre-heat the oven to 200°C/400°F/Gas Mark 6, and place a baking tray in the oven to heat up. Fill the prepared pastry case with the apple mixture. Roll out the remaining pastry to make a lid, moistening the pastry edges and pressing them well together to seal. Place the pie tin on the pre-heated baking sheet in the oven and bake for about 30-40 minutes, until the pastry is crisp and golden (placing it on the hot baking sheet will help the pastry base to cook). Sprinkle the top of the pie with caster sugar and return to the oven for the last few minutes of the cooking time, so that the sugar melts and forms a glaze.

—·—

RECIPE

— · —

Malvern Apple Pudding

This is another traditional apple pudding recipe from Worcestershire, this time from the Malvern area. This dish is traditionally made with Russet apples, which are deliciously sweet, but any small sweet eating apples can be used.

> 115g/4oz butter or margarine
> 115g/4oz sugar
> 2 eggs, beaten
> 115g/4oz plain flour
> A pinch of salt
> 225g/8oz Russet apples, peeled, cored and chopped into small pieces
> Grated rind of 1 lemon
> 50g/2oz currants
> 2-3 tablespoonfuls of brandy (or sherry, if preferred)

Cream together the butter or margarine and the sugar, until light and fluffy. Gradually beat in the beaten eggs, a little at a time, adding a little of the flour if necessary, to prevent curdling. Fold in the flour and salt. Mix the chopped apple with the lemon rind, currants and brandy (or sherry), and fold this into the mixture.

Grease a 1.2 litre (2 pint) pudding basin, and cover the bottom of the pudding basin with a small square of greased greaseproof paper – this will help make the pudding easier to turn out. Put the pudding mixture into the basin. Cover the basin with a lid of pleated greaseproof paper and then a lid of foil, then tie down firmly with string. Place the pudding basin on a trivet or an upturned saucer in a large saucepan. Pour enough boiling water into the pan to come halfway up the sides of the basin. Place the pan on heat and bring the water back to the boil, then cover the pan with its lid and steam the pudding for about 1½ hours, replenishing the pan with more boiling water when necessary, so that it does not boil dry.

When cooked, turn out the pudding onto a warmed serving dish and serve with custard, cream or a brandy or sherry sauce.

— · —

Great Malvern, The Malvern Hills and Wynds Point c1900   7071b

RECITE

— · —

White Ladies Pudding

This traditional recipe from Worcestershire was named after the village of White Ladies Aston near Worcester. Both the village and recipe derived their name from the white habits worn by Cistercian nuns living in a convent in the village in the Middle Ages.

6 medium-thick slices of white bread
75g/3oz butter or margarine
115g/4oz desiccated coconut
600ml/1 pint milk
A pinch of salt
Vanilla essence
3 eggs
75g/3oz sugar

Remove the crusts from the bread. Butter each slice thickly, then cut the slices into squares or triangles. Use the remaining butter to grease a large pie dish. Sprinkle the greased sides of the pie dish with the desiccated coconut, then arrange the bread pieces in the dish. Heat the milk, but do not boil, and add the salt and a few drops of vanilla essence. In a bowl, beat the eggs with the sugar. Pour on the hot milk, stirring all the time to dissolve the sugar, then strain the mixture into the pie dish. Leave to soak, for about 30 minutes.

Pre-heat the oven to 160°C/325°F/Gas Mark 3. Stand the pie dish in a deep-sided roasting tin, and pour in enough hot water to come halfway up the sides of the pie dish. Bake in the middle of the pre-heated oven for about 1½ hours, until the pudding is set. When cooked, turn out the pudding onto a warmed dish. This can be eaten either hot or cold.

— · —

RECIPE

—·—

Fill Belly Pudding

This is a traditional bread pudding recipe from the Black Country that is also a good way of using up stale bread. It can be eaten either as a pudding course or cut into squares and eaten like cake.

450g/1 lb stale bread
1 egg
115g/4oz suet
25g/1oz butter or margarine
225g/8oz granulated or brown sugar
1 level teaspoonful mixed spice
225g/8oz mixed dried fruit

Pre-heat the oven to 160°C/325°F/Gas Mark 3. Soak the bread in water for 10 minutes, then drain and squeeze out the excess moisture. Mash the bread with a fork, then add the remaining ingredients, mix well together and spread the mixture into a greased baking tin. Dot the surface with small knobs of butter, and bake in the pre-heated oven for about 2 hours, until nicely browned. Dredge some more sugar over the surface, and cut into squares to serve. This can be eaten either hot with custard or cream, or cold.

—·—

RECIPE

— · —

Staffordshire Yeomanry Pudding

For the sweet shortcrust pastry:
1 egg yolk
25g/1oz caster sugar
3 teaspoonfuls of cold water
225g/8oz plain flour
Half a level teaspoonful of salt
150g/5oz butter or margarine

For the filling:
115g/4oz butter or margarine
115g/4oz caster sugar
¼ teaspoonful almond essence
25g/1oz ground almonds
2 eggs, separated (only 2 yolks and
  1 white are needed)
2 tablespoonfuls of raspberry jam

First, make the sweet pastry. Mix together the egg yolk, sugar and water. Place the flour and salt in a bowl and rub in the butter or margarine. Add the egg, sugar and water mixture, and mix it all to a firm dough. Knead lightly until the dough is smooth and pliable, then place in the fridge to rest for 15 minutes.

Make the filling whilst the pastry dough is resting. Cream the butter and sugar until light and fluffy, then mix in the almond essence and the ground almonds. Beat the 2 egg yolks and 1 egg white together, then beat into the mixture.

Pre-heat the oven to 180°C/350°F/Gas Mark 4.

Roll out two thirds of the pastry on a lightly-floured surface and use it to line a shallow pie dish or tin. Spread the base with the jam, then pour in the filling mixture. Roll out the remaining pastry and use it to make a lid for the pudding, moistening the edges of the pastry and pressing firmly together to seal. Prick the lid of the pudding with a fork, to make holes for steam to escape. Bake in the pre-heated oven for 40 minutes – the pastry browns very quickly, so you may need to cover the pudding with foil for the last 10 minutes or so to prevent it burning. This should be allowed to cool slightly before eating, but is also very good eaten cold.

— · —

Uttoxeter, Men in the Market Place
c1955 U29012x

Cadbury's

The famous Cadbury's chocolate business was started in 1824 when John Cadbury opened a shop at 93 Bull Street in the centre of Birmingham to sell coffee, tea, cocoa and drinking chocolate. John Cadbury was a member of the Society of Friends, or Quakers as they were commonly called. Quakers were anti alcohol, seeing it as the cause of misery and deprivation in society, and John Cadbury offered his hot drinks as non-alcoholic alternatives for ordinary people.

Situated just south of Birmingham is Bournville, which was chosen by John Cadbury's sons Richard and George Cadbury, also Quakers, in the late 19th century as the site for their new cocoa and chocolate factory and for a model village for their workers. Attached to the present-day factory is Cadbury World, where an exhibition tells the story of the history and manufacture of chocolate.

"*Afternoon Cocoa.*"

In enervating Summer weather something more is required than a drink that is only temporarily refreshing. CADBURY's COCOA undoubtedly supplies the need—being a delicious, refreshing beverage; thin in fluid, highly nutritious, and most sustaining—repairing waste resulting from oppressive heat. It is a perfect drink and food combined. CADBURY's is the ideal beverage for all times and seasons. It is absolutely Pure, therefore the Best Cocoa.

RECIPE

—.—

Quaker's Chocolate Pudding

115g/4oz butter or margarine

115g/4oz plain chocolate

150ml/ ¼ pint milk

115g/4oz fresh breadcrumbs

75g/3oz caster sugar

A few drops of vanilla essence

3 eggs, separated

Melt the butter or margarine with the chocolate in a small saucepan. Add the milk and the breadcrumbs, stir well and leave to cook gently for 10 minutes, stirring occasionally, then remove from heat and allow to cool slightly. Beat in the sugar and the vanilla essence, then beat the egg yolks into the chocolate mixture. Whisk the egg whites until they are stiff and stand in peaks, then fold them into the chocolate mixture, using a large metal spoon.

Grease a 1.2 litre (2 pint) pudding basin, and fill it with the pudding mixture. Cover the pudding basin with a lid of pleated greaseproof paper, and then another of foil, and tie down firmly with string. Place the pudding basin on a trivet or an upturned saucer in a large saucepan. Pour enough boiling water into the pan to come halfway up the sides of the basin. Place the pan on heat and bring the water back to the boil, then cover the pan with its lid and steam the pudding for about 1 hour, replenishing the pan with more boiling water when necessary, so that it does not boil dry.

When cooked, turn out the pudding on to a warmed serving dish, and serve with cream or chocolate sauce.

—.—

RECIPE

— . —

Bilberry and Apple Pie

Eleven miles south-west of the centre of Birmingham are the Lickey Hills, a country park area in Worcestershire. 'The Lickeys' and much of the area around Rednall would have been built on in the 1880s, had it not been for the intervention of the Birmingham Association for the Preservation of Open Spaces. They managed to save 32 acres of countryside from the developers, and the land was later acquired by the Birmingham Corporation and opened to the public. Edward and George Cadbury of Bournville provided additional funds for the purchase of the adjoining Bilberry Hill, which is named after the extensive tracts of bilberry bushes (Vaccinium myrtillus) that grow over much of the hill. For hundreds of years, local people and visitors to the area have cropped the bushes of their free fruit each autumn, to make jams, preserves or bilberry pies. Bilberries grow on small bushes close to the ground and are hard work to pick, but are worth the effort. If you don't want to pick your own bilberries to make this pie, use commercially grown blueberries instead.

> 450g/1 lb bilberries (or blueberries)
> 2 cooking apples
> 225g/8oz sugar
> 1 egg, beaten
> 350g/12oz sweet shortcrust or puff pastry, whichever is preferred

Heat the oven to 200°C/400°F/Gas Mark 6. Remove the cores from the apples with an apple corer, but do not peel them. Stand the apples in an ovenproof dish, add 2 tablespoonfuls of water to the dish and bake in the pre-heated oven for 40-45 minutes, until the apples are tender. When cooked, scrape out the pulp from the apples and mix it with the bilberries and the sugar. Roll out half the pastry on a lightly floured board and use it to line a greased 20cm (8 inch) pie tin. Turn out the fruit mixture into the pie tin. Roll out the remaining pastry to make a lid and place it over the pie, and trim and seal the edges. Brush the lid of the pie with beaten egg white and sprinkle with sugar. Place in the pre-heated oven and bake for ten minutes, then reduce the heat to 180°C/350°F/Gas Mark 4 and cook for a further 30 minutes until the pastry is golden brown and crisp.

— . —

RECITE

—·—

Warwickshire Pudding

115g/4oz butter or margarine

75g/3oz caster sugar

3 eggs, beaten

225g/8oz plain flour

300ml/ ½ pint milk

350g/12oz raspberry jam

Cream the eggs and sugar together until light and fluffy. Gradually add the beaten eggs, a little at a time, adding a little flour if necessary to prevent curdling. Mix in the flour and milk, to make a batter.

Grease a 1.2 litre (2 pint) pudding basin, and line the base with 225g (8oz) of the jam. Pour in the batter. Cover the pudding basin with a lid of pleated greaseproof paper, and then another of foil, and tie down firmly with string. Place the pudding basin on a trivet or an upturned saucer in a large saucepan. Pour enough boiling water into the pan to come halfway up the sides of the basin. Place the pan on heat and bring the water back to the boil, then cover the pan with its lid and steam the pudding for about 1½ hours, replenishing the pan with more boiling water when necessary, so that it does not boil dry.

When the pudding is cooked, warm the remaining jam, turn out the pudding onto a warmed serving dish and serve with the warmed jam poured over the top.

—·—

Rugby, Market Place 1932 85177

TEATIME AND BAKING

Pikelets, or pyclets if you prefer, are popular all over the West Midlands region, but the argument over whether they are the same thing as crumpets, and whether or not they should be cooked in a metal ring to contain the batter, seems to be a question of your own family tradition. However, for many people it is crumpets that are cooked with the batter contained in a special metal ring on the pan or griddle, and pikelets which are cooked as spoonfuls of batter dropped on to the pan or griddle – thus pikelets are thinner than crumpets, and are not cooked into an even round shape, as crumpets are. Whether you call them pikelets or crumpets, the top surface of these yeasted doughy delicacies becomes covered with holes during the cooking process. When you spread them with butter, hot from the pan, the melted butter oozes into the holes – perfect for winter teatimes!

Walsall, The Bridge 1908 W161001

RECIPE

— . —

Pikelets

This recipe uses dried yeast, but if you can find fresh yeast, use 15g/ ½ oz and cream it with a little sugar and some of the warmed water, then leave in a warm place to activate and go frothy before using. This quantity makes about 12 pikelets.

450g/1 lb plain flour (strong white breadmaking flour is best)
350ml/12 fl oz milk, warmed
350ml/12 fl oz water, warmed
7g/ ¼ oz powdered dried yeast (about one small sachet of dried
   breadmaking yeast)
2 level teaspoonfuls salt
1 teaspoonful caster sugar
1 level teaspoonful baking powder
A little sunflower or vegetable oil for greasing the pan or griddle

Place the flour, sugar and dried yeast into a bowl and make a well in the centre. Pour in the warmed water and milk (add the yeast mixture now, if using fresh yeast). Gradually stir the flour into the liquid until you have a creamy batter with no lumps, and beat it well. Cover the bowl with cling film and leave in a warm place for at least an hour until the batter has risen and is bubbly.

Lightly grease a frying pan or griddle (and crumpet rings if using), and place on a medium to high heat. Whisk the salt and the baking powder into the batter. When the pan is hot, drop a good tablespoonful of the mixture into the pan and cook for about five minutes, or if using crumpet rings, place a ring in the pan and drop in enough mixture to fill to just below the top. Lots of holes should form on the surface of the pikelet as it cooks – if not, the mixture is too thick, so whisk some more water into the batter mix before making more. Cook the pikelet on one side for about 5 minutes until the surface is just set, then flip it over (or take it out of the ring and turn it) and cook the other side for about 2 minutes, until it is golden. When each pikelet is cooked, remove it from the pan and keep warm whilst you cook the rest of the batter. Either eat at once whilst they are hot, spread with butter, or cool on a wire tray and keep for toasting later.

— . —

RECIPE

— . —

Stourport Potato Cakes

This recipe from Stourport-on-Severn in north Worcestershire makes sweet, spicy small cakes for teatime

2 generous cups of mashed potato
4 heaped tablespoonfuls of self-raising flour
2 tablespoonfuls of brown sugar
25g/1oz melted butter
A pinch of ginger or cinnamon, whichever is preferred
150ml/ ¼ pint of milk

Mix together all the dry ingredients and the potato. Add the melted butter, and mix it all to a stiff dough with the milk. Place the dough on a lightly-floured surface and knead until it is smooth.

Roll out the dough to about 2cm (1 inch) thick, and cut it into rounds with a biscuit cutter.

The potato cakes can either be baked on both sides on a greased griddle, or placed on a greased baking sheet and baked in a hot oven (200°C/400°F/Gas Mark 6) for 20 minutes.

Serve the potato cakes hot, as soon as possible after cooking, spread with butter.

— . —

RECITE

— · —

Cider Cake

Herefordshire has been renowned for centuries as a cider-producing area. When John Wycliffe translated the Bible into English around 1420, his assistant, Nicholas of Hereford, translated the words 'strong drink' in St John's Gospel as 'cider', reflecting the prevalence of cider as the main form of alcohol locally available. This version of the Bible is known as 'The Cider Bible', and a copy can be seen in the chained library at Hereford Cathedral, the finest chained library in the world, containing books and manuscripts that date back a thousand years or more. Chaining the books was an important form of security, enabling people to read the precious books on the ledge below, while ensuring they could not be taken away. There are still 10,000 acres of orchards in Herefordshire where many different varieties of apple are grown, which are mixed together to produce juice for the county's famous cider.

225g/8oz mixed sultanas, raisins and currants

4 tablespoonfuls sweet or medium Herefordshire cider

175g/6oz butter or margarine

175g/6oz soft brown sugar

3 eggs

225g/8oz self-raising flour

1 teaspoonful mixed spice

Soak the dried fruit in the cider overnight. Pre-heat the oven to 180°C/350°F/Gas Mark 4. Cream the butter or margarine, add the sugar and cream until fluffy. Lightly beat the eggs and gradually beat them into the mixture, a little at a time, adding a little of the flour to prevent curdling. Mix in the fruit and the cider. Sift the flour and mixed spice together, fold in half of the flour, and mix well, then mix in the rest of the flour. Grease a 20cm (8 inch) round or 18cm (7 inch) square tin and line the bottom with greased, greaseproof paper. Turn the mixture into the prepared tin and bake in the pre-heated moderate oven for about 1 hour and 15 minutes.

— · —

RECIPE

—·—

Coventry Godcakes

A 'godcake' is sometimes used in Warwickshire and West Midlands as a name for the triangle of grass at a road junction that is created as the road splits to go left and right. The name refers to the triangular-shaped pastry cakes known as Godcakes which were traditionally given by godparents in the Coventry area to their godchildren on New Year's Eve, for good luck. The child received both a blessing and a cake from the godparent, but the size of the cakes could vary, depending on the wealth and generosity of the giver!

225g/8oz puff pastry
115g/4oz mincemeat
1 egg white, beaten
2 teaspoonfuls rum or brandy (optional)
Caster sugar

Pre-heat the oven to 220°C/425°F/Gas Mark 7.

Roll out the pastry thinly on a lightly floured surface. Cut the pastry into 10cm (4 inch) squares, then cut each square in half on the diagonal to produce two triangles.

Mix the mincemeat with the rum or brandy if used, then place a small spoonful of mincemeat in the middle of half the pastry triangles – don't be too generous with the mixture or it will spill out from the sides of the cakes when the 'lids' are added. Moisten the edges of the triangles with a little water, then cover each filled triangle with a second triangle on top, pressing down firmly to seal the edges.

Cut three small diagonal slashes across the top of each Godcake with a sharp knife (some traditions say that these represent the Holy Trinity of Christian belief), then brush the top of each cake with beaten egg white and sprinkle with caster sugar. Place the Godcakes on a greased baking sheet and bake for about 15 minutes, or until golden and well puffed up. Cool on a wire rack and eat as soon as possible!

—·—

Coventry, St Mary's Hall 1892 30929

RECIPE

—·—

Simnel Cake

Simnel Cake is a light fruit cake traditionally eaten at Easter, although originally Simnel Cakes were eaten on Mothering Sunday. England has several recipes for Simnel Cake, but the version that originated in Shrewsbury in Shropshire has become the best known; this has eleven marzipan balls on the top, representing the true apostles of Jesus, omitting Judas, the twelfth, who betrayed him.

For the marzipan (or ready-made marzipan can be used if preferred):
450g/1 lb ground almonds
450g/1 lb icing sugar
Half a teaspoonful almond essence
1 tablespoonful lemon juice
4 egg yolks

For the cake:
175g/6oz butter or margarine
175g/6oz caster sugar
3 eggs, beaten
225g/8oz self-raising flour, sifted
1 teaspoonful ground cinnamon
1 teaspoonful ground nutmeg
1 teaspoonful mixed spice
Pinch of salt
350g/12oz currants
115g/4oz sultanas
75g/3oz candied peel, chopped
A little milk to mix
2 tablespoonfuls apricot jam, warmed

Mix the marzipan ingredients to a stiff paste and knead well; divide into three and roll out two of the pieces into circles to fit the cake tin used (see below). Put aside with the rest of the marzipan.
To make the cake, cream the butter or margarine and sugar together until light and fluffy, then beat in the eggs a little at a time. Sieve the flour, spices and salt together and add to the mixture, and finally add the dried fruit and peel. If the mixture is a little stiff, add enough milk to give a dropping consistency. Put half the cake mixture into a greased and lined cake tin 18-20cm (7-8 inches) round, then put in one circle of marzipan and cover with the remaining cake mixture. Bake slowly in a pre-heated oven at 150°C/300°F/Gas Mark 2, for 3½ hours.

Allow the cake to cool, then brush the top with a little warmed apricot jam, and put on the second circle of marzipan, pressing down well. Make eleven small balls from the remaining marzipan, and arrange these around the edge of the top of the cake, fixing with dabs of jam. Brush lightly with a little beaten egg, and put the cake in a hot oven or under the grill for a few seconds to glaze lightly.

—·—

RECIPE

—·—

Shrewsbury Biscuits

These tasty fruited biscuits, flavoured with lemon and cinnamon, are much nicer when they are home-made!

> 225g/8oz self-raising flour
> 115g/4oz butter or margarine
> 115g/4oz caster sugar
> 1 egg yolk
> Grated lemon rind
> Pinch of salt
> Half a teaspoonful of powdered cinnamon
> 50g/2oz currants

Pre-heat the oven to 140°C/275°F/Gas Mark 1. Cream together the butter and sugar until light and fluffy. Sift the flour and salt together. Add the egg yolk to the creamed butter and sugar with a tablespoonful of flour and beat well. Fold in the remaining flour, cinnamon, currants and lemon rind. Roll out the dough on a lightly floured surface to about 5mm (¼ inch) thick. Cut into rounds, and place them on a greased baking tray. Bake in the pre-heated oven for 20 minutes. Allow to cool on the baking tray for a few minutes, then turn on to a wire rack.

—·—

Shrewsbury 1923 73812

RECIPE

—.—

Staffordshire Oatcakes

Staffordshire Oatcakes are similar to pancakes but are made with oatmeal, and are served rolled up and filled with either sweet or savoury fillings. Try them with ham, bacon, mushrooms, grated cheese, egg, and sausage, or for a quick snack wrapped around cheese and warmed in a microwave or under a grill, or eat them whilst still warm from the pan, spread with honey, jam or golden syrup.

> 475g/1 lb 4oz medium/pinhead oatmeal
> 350g/12oz strong white plain flour
> 3 tablespoonfuls dried skimmed milk powder
> 4 teaspoonfuls quick acting dried yeast
> 2 teaspoonfuls sugar
> Oil for frying

Place all ingredients into large bowl and make a well in centre. Add 1 litre (1¾ pints) of warm water and mix well (the mixture should be quite thin, like pancake batter). Cover the bowl and leave it in a warm place such as an airing cupboard for about 1½ - 2 hours. After standing, uncover and mix well, adding more water if necessary to loosen the batter – up to 600ml (1 pint) more if necessary. Add 2 teaspoonfuls of salt at this stage.

Heat a griddle or large frying pan, and use about 1 teaspoonful of oil to fry each oatcake. Pour enough batter into the pan to cover the base, making the oatcakes as thick as you prefer them, rolling the pan to get an even coverage, and turn each oatcake once so that it is cooked on both sides.

—.—

One of the most famous landmarks in Stafford is the four-storey, half-timbered High House, which was built around 1595 by the wealthy Dorrington family. During the Civil War of the 17th century King Charles I and Prince Rupert had their quarters in the house during the King's march from Derby to Shrewsbury in September 1642, but later in that conflict the house was used as a prison for Royalist officers. During the 1780s it was occupied by Dr Thomas Fowler, a physician at the Infirmary. He developed an arsenic solution to treat patients with 'agues, remitting fevers and periodic headaches'. As 'Fowlers Solution' it became a popular medicine in Victorian times, and was used to treat everything from asthma to rheumatism, as well as being used as a cosmetic face wash!

Stafford, The Ancient High House 1948 S411010

RECIPE

— . —

Kidderminster Plum Cakes

This recipe comes from Kidderminster in Worcestershire. Although these are called plum cakes, they are actually made with a mixture of dried fruit – currants, raisins and sultanas

> 4 glacé cherries
> 225g/8oz mixed dried fruit – currants, raisins, sultanas
> 50g/2oz plain flour
> 50g/2oz soft brown sugar
> 50g/2oz butter or margarine
> 1 egg
> Half a teaspoonful mixed spice
> 375g/13oz packet of puff pastry
> Granulated sugar, to finish

Pre-heat the oven to 200°C/400°F/Gas Mark 6.

Roughly chop the glacé cherries and put them in a bowl with the rest of the filling ingredients. Mix together thoroughly for about 3 minutes, beating the mixture hard with a wooden spoon.

If you have bought frozen puff pastry, allow it to thaw just before making these cakes. Roll out the pastry very thin on a lightly floured surface, and cut it into rounds about 10cm (4 inches) in diameter – this should make about 12 rounds. Place 2 teaspoonfuls of the filling into the centre of each round. Brush the edges of the pastry rounds with water, and gather up the edges of each round over the filling, and press the edges together well to seal them. Turn each plum cake over so the join is underneath, and roll each cake lightly with a rolling pin, to give them a flattened round shape. Brush the top of each cake with water, sprinkle them liberally with granulated sugar and press the sugar on firmly to give them a thick sugary coating.

 Place the cakes on a greased baking sheet, and cut three slashes across the top of each cake with a sharp knife. Bake in the pre-heated oven for about 20 minutes, until the cakes are golden brown, then cool on a wire rack.

— . —

A Priest Hole in the Kitchen

A few miles from Kidderminster is Harvington Hall, a wonderful example of an Elizabethan timber-framed and brick building. It was built in the 1580s by Humphrey Pakington – he was a Roman Catholic and this was an era when religious persecution of Catholics was rife. It was against the law for priests to say Mass, and a treasonable offence for anyone to shelter Roman Catholic priests within England. The huge fireplace in the kitchen of Harvington Hall is of particular interest because behind the Elizabethan bread oven (left of the kitchen range) is a hiding place known as a priest hole, where Jesuit priests could hide. At Harvington Hall there are four of these priest holes.

Kidderminster, Harvington Hall, The Kitchen c1965 K16088

Market Drayton, Market Day 1911 63338

Souling

In many parts of England in earlier times November 1st, or All Souls' Eve, was when families remembered the souls of departed relatives, which were thought to return to their homes on this night – sometimes bonfires would be lit on the hills to light their way home. Prayers were said for the dead, and food was left on kitchen tables in the night. On All Souls' Day on November 2nd, 'souling' would also take place, when 'soulers' would travel from door to door begging for soul-cakes in return for songs and prayers for the dead. In Shropshire the children who went souling would sing a special rhyme in return for a spiced cake marked with a cross:

A soul-cake, a soul-cake, please,
Good missus, a soul-cake.
One for Peter, two for Paul,
Three for Him who saved us all.

Wellington, New Street 1907 58919

RECIPE

— . —

Shropshire Soul Cakes

175g/6oz butter
175g/6oz caster sugar
3 egg yolks
450g/1 lb self-raising flour
A pinch of salt
1 teaspoonful ground mixed spice
Half a teaspoonful ground ginger
75g/3oz currants
About 2 tablespoonfuls milk
Extra caster sugar, to finish

Pre-heat the oven to 180°C/350°F/Gas Mark 4.

Cream together the butter and sugar until light and fluffy, then beat in the egg yolks. Sift together the flour, salt, mixed spice and ginger and fold it into the egg mixture with the currants, adding just enough milk to form a soft dough.

Lightly roll out the dough on a floured surface to about 5mm (¼ inch) thick. Cut into small rounds with a biscuit cutter, about 7.5cm (3 inches) in diameter. Place the rounds on greased baking sheets. Prick the surfaces of the rounds lightly with a fork, then mark a deep cross across the top of each cake, using the back of a knife.

Bake in the pre-heated oven for about 15 minutes, until the cakes are risen and golden brown. Remove from the oven and leave on the baking trays for a few minutes, then sprinkle the cakes with a little caster sugar and cool on a wire rack.

— . —

Ludlow
The Feathers Hotel
1892 30829

INDEX OF PHOTOGRAPHS

INDEX OF RECIPES

FREE PRINT OF YOUR CHOICE

Mounted Print
Overall size 14 x 11 inches (355 x 280mm)

Choose any Frith photograph in this book.
Simply complete the Voucher opposite and return it with your remittance for £3.50 (to cover postage and handling) and we will print the photograph of your choice in SEPIA (size 11 x 8 inches) and supply it in a cream mount with a burgundy rule line (overall size 14 x 11 inches).
Please note: aerial photographs and photographs with a reference number starting with a "Z" are not Frith photographs and cannot be supplied under this offer. Offer valid for delivery to one UK address only.

PLUS: **Order additional Mounted Prints at HALF PRICE - £10.00 each** (normally £20.00)
If you would like to order more Frith prints from this book, possibly as gifts for friends and family, you can buy them at half price (with no additional postage and handling costs).

PLUS: **Have your Mounted Prints framed**
For an extra £19.00 per print you can have your mounted print(s) framed in an elegant polished wood and gilt moulding, overall size 16 x 13 inches (no additional postage and handling required).

IMPORTANT!

These special prices are only available if you use this form to order. You must use the ORIGINAL VOUCHER on this page (no copies permitted). We can only despatch to one UK address. This offer cannot be combined with any other offer.

Send completed Voucher form to:
The Francis Frith Collection, Unit 6, Oakley Business Park, Wylye Road, Dinton, Wiltshire SP3 5EU

CHOOSE A PHOTOGRAPH FROM THIS BOOK

Voucher for **FREE** *and Reduced Price Frith Prints*

Please do not photocopy this voucher. Only the original is valid, so please fill it in, cut it out and return it to us with your order.

Picture ref no	Page no	Qty	Mounted @ £10.00	Framed + £19.00	Total Cost £
		1	Free of charge*	£	£
			£10.00	£	£
			£10.00	£	£
			£10.00	£	£
			£10.00	£	£
			£10.00	£	£

Please allow 28 days for delivery. Offer available to one UK address only

	* Post & handling	£3.50
	Total Order Cost	£

Title of this book . . . .

I enclose a cheque/postal order for £ . . . .
made payable to 'The Francis Frith Collection'

OR please debit my Mastercard / Visa / Maestro card, details below

Card Number:

Issue No (Maestro only):   Valid from (Maestro):

Card Security Number: Expires:

Signature:

Name Mr/Mrs/Ms . . . .

Address . . . .

. . . .

. . . .

. . . . Postcode . . . .

Daytime Tel No . . . .

Email . . . .

Valid to 31/12/14

Free Print – see overleaf

Can you help us with information about any of the Frith photographs in this book?

We are gradually compiling an historical record for each of the photographs in the Frith archive. It is always fascinating to find out the names of the people shown in the pictures, as well as insights into the shops, buildings and other features depicted.

If you recognize anyone in the photographs in this book, or if you have information not already included in the author's caption, do let us know. We would love to hear from you, and will try to publish it in future books or articles.

An Invitation from The Francis Frith Collection to Share Your Memories

The 'Share Your Memories' feature of our website allows members of the public to add personal memories relating to the places featured in our photographs, or comment on others already added. Seeing a place from your past can rekindle forgotten or long held memories. Why not visit the website, find photographs of places you know well and add YOUR story for others to read and enjoy? We would love to hear from you!

www.francisfrith.com/memories

Our production team

Frith books are produced by a small dedicated team at offices near Salisbury. Most have worked with the Frith Collection for many years. All have in common one quality: they have a passion for the Frith Collection.

Frith Books and Gifts

We have a wide range of books and gifts available on our website utilising our photographic archive, many of which can be individually personalised.

www.francisfrith.com

FRITH PRODUCTS & SERVICES

Francis Frith would doubtless be pleased to know that the pioneering publishing venture he started in 1860 still continues today. Over a hundred and forty years later, The Francis Frith Collection continues in the same innovative tradition and is now one of the foremost publishers of vintage photographs in the world. Some of the current activities include:

INTERIOR DECORATION

Today Frith's photographs can be seen framed and as giant wall murals in thousands of pubs, restaurants, hotels, banks, retail stores and other public buildings throughout the country. In every case they enhance the unique local atmosphere of the places they depict and provide reminders of gentler days in an increasingly busy and frenetic world.

PRODUCT PROMOTIONS

Frith products are used by many major companies to promote the sales of their own products or to reinforce their own history and heritage. Frith promotions have been used by Hovis bread, Courage beers, Scots Porage Oats, Colman's mustard, Cadbury's foods, Mellow Birds coffee, Dunhill pipe tobacco, Guinness, and Bulmer's Cider.

GENEALOGY AND FAMILY HISTORY

As the interest in family history and roots grows world-wide, more and more people are turning to Frith's photographs of Great Britain for images of the towns, villages and streets where their ancestors lived; and, of course, photographs of the churches and chapels where their ancestors were christened, married and buried are an essential part of every genealogy tree and family album.

FRITH PRODUCTS

All Frith photographs are available Framed or just as Mounted Prints and Posters (size 23 x 16 inches). These may be ordered from the address below. Other products available are - Address Books, Calendars, Jigsaws, Canvas Prints, Postcards and local and prestige books.

THE INTERNET

Already ninety thousand Frith photographs can be viewed and purchased on the internet through the Frith websites and a myriad of partner sites.

For more detailed information on Frith products, look at this site:
www.francisfrith.com

See the complete list of Frith Books at: www.francisfrith.com
This web site is regularly updated with the latest list of publications from The Francis Frith Collection. If you wish to buy books relating to another part of the country that your local bookshop does not stock, you may purchase on-line.

For further information, trade, or author enquiries please contact us at the address below:
The Francis Frith Collection, 6 Oakley Business Park, Wylye Road, Dinton, Wiltshire SP3 5EU.
Tel: +44 (0)1722 716 376 Fax: +44 (0)1722 716 881 Email: sales@francisfrith.co.uk

---

See Frith products on the internet at www.francisfrith.com

FREE PRINT OF YOUR CHOICE
CHOOSE A PHOTOGRAPH FROM THIS BOOK

+ £3.80 POSTAGE

Mounted Print
Overall size 14 x 11 inches (355 x 280mm)

TO RECEIVE YOUR FREE PRINT

Choose any Frith photograph in this book

Simply complete the Voucher opposite and return it with your remittance for £3.80 (to cover postage and handling) and we will print the photograph of your choice in SEPIA (size 11 x 8 inches) and supply it in a cream mount ready to frame (overall size 14 x 11 inches).

Order additional Mounted Prints
at HALF PRICE - £12.00 each (normally £24.00)

If you would like to order more Frith prints from this book, possibly as gifts for friends and family, you can buy them at half price (with no additional postage costs).

Have your Mounted Prints framed

For an extra £20.00 per print you can have your mounted print(s) framed in an elegant polished wood and gilt moulding, overall size 16 x 13 inches (no additional postage required).

IMPORTANT!

❶ Please note: aerial photographs and photographs with a reference number starting with a "Z" are not Frith photographs and cannot be supplied under this offer.

❷ Offer valid for delivery to one UK address only.

❸ These special prices are only available if you use this form to order. You must use the ORIGINAL VOUCHER on this page (no copies permitted). We can only despatch to one UK address.

❹ This offer cannot be combined with any other offer.

As a customer your name & address will be stored by Frith but not sold or rented to third parties. Your data will be used for the purpose of this promotion only.

Send completed Voucher form to:

The Francis Frith Collection,
19 Kingsmead Business Park, Gillingham,
Dorset SP8 5FB

Voucher for *FREE* and *Reduced Price Frith Prints*

Please do not photocopy this voucher. Only the original is valid, so please fill it in, cut it out and return it to us with your order.

Picture ref no	Page no	Qty	Mounted @ £12.00	Framed + £20.00	Total Cost £
		1	Free of charge*	£	£
			£12.00	£	£
			£12.00	£	£
			£12.00	£	£
			£12.00	£	£
			£12.00	£	£

Please allow 28 days for delivery.
Offer available to one UK address only

* Post & handling	£3.80
Total Order Cost	£

Title of this book . . . .

I enclose a cheque/postal order for £ . . . .
made payable to 'The Francis Frith Collection'

OR please debit my Mastercard / Visa / Maestro card, details below

Card Number:

Issue No (Maestro only):   Valid from (Maestro):

Card Security Number: Expires:

Signature:

Name Mr/Mrs/Ms . . . .

Address . . . .

. . . .

. . . .

. . . . Postcode . . . .

Daytime Tel No . . . .

Email . . . .

Valid to 31/12/18